Ask Me About Animals

By Sally Cowan

You can ask me anything about animals!
I know a lot.

I even made a book with all my best animal facts!

Making a book is a big task.
First, I had to write a draft, and then find some photos.

I hope you like it!

Animals live all over our vast planet.

Some animals are big, and some are small.

Some are fast, and some are slow.

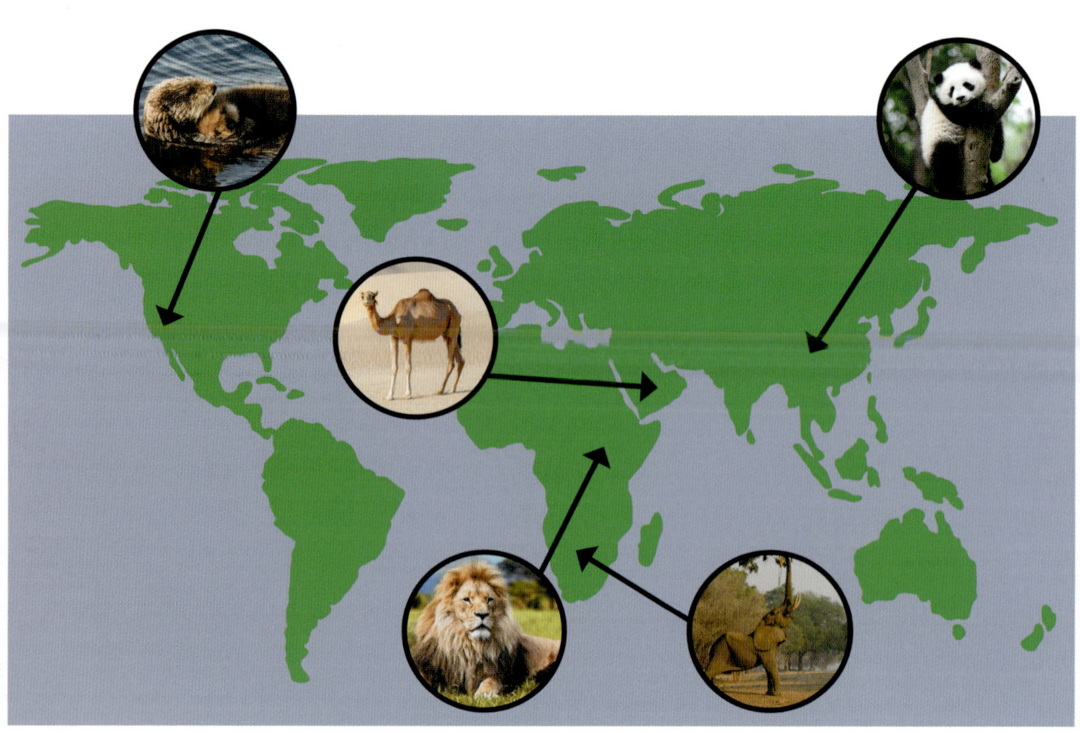

Huge elephants live in hot places.

They eat **lots** of grass and grasp leaves from trees with their long trunks.

Camels can live in hot, dry places called deserts.

They can walk across hot sand with their padded feet.
Long eyelashes protect their eyes from blasts of wind.

Camels can last a long time without water.

Some camels live in cold places.

There is not much grass to eat, so the camels keep extra fat in their humps.
They use the fat like food when there is no grass.

Sea otters live in wet places.
They grow fur that keeps
them dry!

This otter mum naps while
floating on her back.
She grasps her sleeping pup.

Otter fathers don't stay with their pups.

Male otters hang out in big groups called rafts.

Pandas are big and slow.

A panda has dark fur around its eyes that looks like a mask.

Pandas pass the time eating and sleeping.
After they sleep, they eat.
And after they eat, they sleep again!

Lions are fast!

They can run across the grassland to catch a zebra or a buffalo.

Turtles are rather slow on land. But they are much faster when they swim!

Some animals come from
distant lands.
And some live right next to you.

I bet you walk past animals
every day!

An animal can even live with you!

CHECKING FOR MEANING

1. What is one thing elephants do with their trunks? *(Literal)*
2. What do camels store in their humps? *(Literal)*
3. Why are turtles faster in the water than they are on land? *(Inferential)*
4. What is your favourite fact that you learned in this book? Why? *(Evaluative)*

EXTENDING VOCABULARY

draft	What is a draft? Why is it best to write a draft first?
vast	What does the author mean when she says the Earth is vast? What is another word she could have used?
distant	What does the word *distant* mean? What is another way the author could have described *distant lands*?

MOVING BEYOND THE TEXT

1. What did you learn about an animal from this book that you didn't already know? What else would you like to know about that animal?

2. What word do we use for an animal that lives with you? How are pets different from the other animals mentioned in the text?

3. If you could travel the world to see any animal, where would you go? What animal would you want to see?

4. Camels live in the desert. What other animals might you find in a desert?

TIME TO WRITE

Write about an animal that you know lots of facts about. What does it look like? Where does it live? What does it eat?